British Cars of the Late Fifties 1955-1959

research by David J. Voller

edited by Bart H. Vanderveen

ISBN 0 85429 571 2

A **FOULIS** Motoring Book

First published, in the Auto Library Series, by Olyslager Organisation, 1975
Reprinted 1981, 1986, 1990

Published by:
Haynes Publishing Group
Sparkford, Nr. Yeovil,
Somerset BA22 7JJ

Haynes Publications Inc,
861 Lawrence Drive, Newbury Park,
California 91320 USA.

Other titles in this series

Trucks of the Sixties and Seventies
Wreckers and Recovery Vehicles

American Cars of the 1930s
American Cars of the 1940s
American Cars of the 1950s
American Cars of the 1960s
American Cars of the 1970s

British Cars of the Early Thirties
British Cars of the Late Thirties
British Cars of the Late Forties
British Cars of the Early Fifties
British Cars of the Early Sixties
British Cars of the Late Sixties

INTRODUCTION

The last five years of the fifties represented a very exciting period in the life of the British Motor Industry, albeit an extremely challenging one. The drive to increase penetration into the increasingly competitive export markets was seen as vital if Britain was to recover her former distinction as the world's leading supplier of motor vehicles. The enormous importance which the industry placed on the Continent of Europe as a lucrative export market was borne out by the marked tendency for the design of British cars to cater more for European tastes, and the greater attention being paid to after-sales service facilities on the Continent. The taxation system in Britain meant that the motor car was still very much a luxury to the majority of home buyers, although by the end of the decade a relaxation in credit restrictions had brought about a marked increase in the number of UK new car registrations. During the period the British Motor Industry produced—and comfortably exceeded—a million cars for the first time in a single year, while, at the same time, introducing some of the most popular and best-loved models ever made. Although the well-known manufacturers had their fair share of problems in helping to achieve this impressive figure, the frequently forgotten 'smaller independents' were battling against often impossible odds to produce motor cars which were 'that bit different'. A number, inevitably, went under—usually due to financial problems, but thankfully there were—and still are—others willing to take up the challenge.

A selection of these cars—some well known, others not so well known—are included along with the more familiar names in this book which is a follow-up to *British Cars of the Early Fifties.*

Piet Olyslager, MSIA, MSAE, KIVI

4A AC Ace

4A : **AC** Ace, unveiled in the autumn of 1953, did not in fact, reach the production stage until later the following year by which time a number of modifications had been made. The headlamps were raised and positioned alongside a recessed, raked-back radiator grille, the alloy body was carried by a stronger tubular frame, cam steering replaced the rack and pinion variety and the suspension layout was revised slightly. Powered by a six-cylinder 1991-cc engine which produced 76 bhp at 4500 rpm, it featured all independent suspension. A two-seater hard-top coupé—the Aceca—was also added (*see* 1956).

4B : **Allard** Safari estate car was mechanically similar to the contemporary Allard P2 Monte Carlo saloon (so named to commemorate Sydney Allard's outright victory in the 1952 Monte Carlo Rally). Both had a Ford V8 engine as standard but other—more powerful—engines could be fitted at extra cost. The Safari had three bench seats, the rearmost facing backwards, and, at 16 ft 6 in, was 6 in longer than the saloon. In October 1955 both models were listed at £2525 12s 6d.

1955

With the memories of the difficult post-war years hopefully beginning to fade, the British motor industry moved into the second half of the fifties intent on keeping and expanding its world trade despite the growing threat of intensive competition from other countries.

After developing and producing a number of small economy saloons during the early fifties, the industry generally seemed to turn its attention to enlarging and improving the larger cars for 1955. Austin replaced their four-cylinder Hereford with the six-cylinder A90 Westminster; Daimler added five new large models to their range; Aston Martin, Bentley, Jaguar and Rolls-Royce increased the power of their engines; Morris introduced the six-cylinder Isis and Wolseley the Six/Ninety.

There was also strong evidence that British manufacturers were beginning to recognize what the Americans had accepted years before—that women have a considerable say where the potential car buyer is concerned.

Sadly a number of car manufacturers went the way of all flesh during the latter part of 1954 or in 1955, namely Lea-Francis, Jowett and Swallow. Lanchester followed soon after.

Of the 905,623 cars produced during the year, 388,564 were exported and 517,059 were UK registrations (including 5,639 hackneys). Imports were, however, more than double the previous year's—11,131 *v.* 4660 cars.

4B Allard Safari

5A Alvis Three Litre TC21-100

5A/B: **Alvis** Three Litre TC21-100 Drophead Coupé was an impressive Tickford-bodied two-door alternative to the Grey Lady four-door Saloon. Both models were fitted with the 2993-cc 100-bhp twin-carburettor engine and featured a sunshine roof (saloon), wire wheels and a pair of additional driving lamps as standard; pressed wheels were optionally available. Body supply problems, alas, meant that the Coupé was discontinued in August 1955—Tickford was acquired about that time by the David Brown group, which made the Aston Martin and Lagonda cars.

5B Alvis Three Litre TC21-100

5C Armstrong Siddeley Sapphire 346

5C: **Armstrong Siddeley** Sapphire 346 luxury saloon, powered by a six-cylinder, 3·4-litre engine. This Mark II version featured a number of modifications including flashing trafficators, rubber stoneguards, larger brake drums, automatic light switches for bonnet and boot and additional dash warning lights; automatic transmission was optionally available. It became the first British car to list power-assisted steering as an optional extra, in the summer of 1955.

5D: **Armstrong Siddeley** Limousine was a long-wheelbase seven/eight-seater version, mechanically similar to the 346 saloon but some 5 cwt heavier, 19 in longer and 2 in higher. Wheelbase was 133 in (114 in on the Saloon). Tyre size was 7.00-16 in.

5D Armstrong Siddeley Limousine

1955

6A/B: **Aston Martin** DB2-4. Available as Sports Saloon and Drophead Coupé, this model was fitted with a 3-litre twin-overhead-camshaft engine, developing 140 bhp at 5000 rpm, from about the middle of 1954. The occasional rear seats, which were suitable mainly for children, could, on the saloon, be folded down to give a long flat luggage platform reached via the top-hinged opening rear panel.

6A Aston Martin DB2-4

6B Aston Martin DB2-4

6C Austin A30 Countryman

6C: **Austin** A30 Model AP4 Countryman. Mechanically similar to the saloon version, this two-door utility model had a squarish metal-panelled body, with a single rear seat. Dimensions: length 11 ft 6 in, width 4 ft 8 in, height 5 ft 3 in. The two-door and four-door saloons were continued with no material changes.

6D: **Austin** A40 Cambridge Saloon, Model GS5. Following on the tradition of the Devon and Somerset A40s, this four-door model—a limited number of two-door models were also built—had a completely new flush-sided body which featured a low, wide grille with five 'rippled' horizontal bars, a dummy air scoop on the bonnet nose. and straight-through wings. Powered by the reliable 1200-cc 42-bhp engine, it had a $6\frac{3}{4}$ in longer wheelbase than its predecessor (the Somerset) and yet was only $2\frac{3}{4}$ in longer overall. Also available was the A50, which was a bigger-engined version—1489 cc, 50 bhp at 4400 rpm.

6D Austin A40 Cambridge

7A Austin A90 Westminster

7B Austin-Healey 100

7A: **Austin** A90 Westminster Model BS4 Saloon had a similar body to the A40/A50 Cambridge but with detail differences such as a seven-bar grille, chrome body-side mouldings and greater overall dimensions. It was powered by a six-cylinder 2639-cc 85-bhp engine coupled with a four-speed gearbox; overdrive or automatic transmission were optional. The A90 was replaced by the A95 in October 1956 (*see* 1957).

7B: **Austin-Healey** 100 Sports. This 2·6-litre engined, sleek, low-contoured sports two-seater was continued from 1954 with no material changes to the standard model specification. Late in 1954, however, a modified version for sports-car racing was evolved, namely the 100S. Apart from the basic body and chassis structure it was virtually a new car, recognizable by its wide shallow oval grille, shallow frameless curved Perspex windscreen and aluminium alloy body panelling. The much-modified power unit gave it a power output of 132 bhp at 4700 rpm. A supercharged development of the 100S, driven by Donald Healey, reached 192·6 mph at the Utah Salt Flats in the United States.

7C/D: **Bentley** Continental. Fitted with a larger engine (4887 cc; previously 4566 cc) this superb model was continued with the addition of two new versions from Park Ward Ltd, namely the Sports Saloon and the Drophead Coupé. The original H. J. Mulliner Saloon was also available. Automatic transmission could be supplied at extra cost on all models.

7C Bentley Continental

7D Bentley Continental

1955

8A: **Bristol** 405 Saloon was the first four-door model produced by the Bristol company. It was similar to the 404 at the front but was considerably longer (15 ft $9\frac{1}{4}$ in *v.* 14 ft $3\frac{1}{4}$ in), giving comfortable seating for four people and was powered by a 1971-cc engine which developed 105 bhp at 5000 rpm. A Drophead Coupé version with coachwork by Abbott of Farnham was also available. The 403 and 404 models were continued until October 1955.

8A Bristol 405

8B: **Citroën** 2CV front-wheel drive car was continued with the introduction of the AZ, which was an improved version of the existing A model. The most important modification was the adoption of a larger engine—425 cc—which raised the output to 12 bhp (was 9 bhp with the A model's 375 cc engine). The A model was discontinued in July 1955.

8C Daimler Regency

8B Citroën 2CV

8C: **Daimler** Regency Mark II DF 304 Saloon was one of five new Daimler models introduced for 1955 and based on variants of two engines and two chassis types. The four-door saloon version shown had a $3\frac{1}{2}$-litre engine; also available was a 4·6-litre version (Series DF400). The two Regency and two Sportsman Saloon models were mounted on a 114-in wheelbase, whereas the Regina seven-seater Limousine had a 130-in wheelbase chassis. The Conquest models were continued.

THE VERSATILE **Dellow** TWO-SEATER

9A Dellow Mark II

9A: **Dellow** Mark II (B and C) Two-Seater was continued from the previous year without any material changes. This Ford-based competition sports model was powered by an 1172-cc engine and featured a body panelled in aluminium, mounted on a stout tubular frame. Also available was a Mark V version, recognizable by an oval air intake with vertical bars, and broad flat bonnet. The Mark IIB was discontinued in 1956.

9B: **Ford** Zephyr Saloon, Model EOTTA, was continued from 1954—together with the convertible version and the Zodiac and Consul (EOTA) saloons and convertibles—with detail modifications. The Zephyr and Zodiac featured a six-cylinder 2262-cc engine which developed 68 bhp (71 bhp on the Zodiac) at 4200 rpm. The Consul had a four-cylinder 1508-cc engine.

9C: **Ford** Zephyr Estate Car, a conversion of the saloon by Abbott of Farnham. Originally the subject of a draughtsman's lunchtime doodle, this 'luggage-locker-extension design' became so popular that cars were soon being converted for export.

9D: **Frazer-Nash** Sebring, an impressive two-seater which was named in honour of the Frazer-Nash victory in the twelve-hour endurance race at Sebring, USA, in 1952, was continued with no material changes. Powered by the famous six-cylinder 2-litre Bristol engine it was developed from the Mark II Competition model. It featured a full-width body of more rounded form, and a low-set lozenge-shaped radiator grille.

9B Ford Zephyr

9C Ford Zephyr

9D Frazer-Nash

1955

10A Hillman Minx Mark VIII

10A: **Hillman** Minx De Luxe Saloon, Convertible (shown) and Californian Hard-top models continued as Mark VIII with a number of modifications including a new 1390-cc 47-bhp overhead-valve engine, restyled radiator grille, sidelamp plinths and flashing trafficators, smaller wheels (15 in *v.* 16 in) and improvements to the suspension. The Special Saloon and the Estate Car retained the 1265-cc side-valve engine (until October). All models had 7 ft 9 in wheelbase. Of the Estate Car there was a Commer 8-cwt van variant.

10B: **Hillman** Husky first appeared in late 1954, for the 1955 model year, as a compact handy little estate car powered by the Minx 1265-cc side-valve engine and fitted with many of its mechanical parts, although it had shorter wheelbase (7 ft) and body. The Husky featured individual front seats, fold-down rear bench seat and a single side-hinged rear door The radiator grille was similar to that of the Minx Mark VIII. This picture was taken on Leith Hill, near Dorking in Surrey. From early 1956 the Husky was also available as a 7-cwt panel van, named Commer Cob.

10B Hillman Husky Mark I

10C: **HRG** 1½-Litre Sports/Racing car. Following on the traditions of this famous sports-car manufacturer in Tolworth, Surrey, but vastly different from its predecessors, this car featured an attractive full-width light-alloy body, braced twin-tube chassis with transverse spring suspension (front and rear), a 1497-cc 108-bhp engine and cast magnesium spider wheels, but never progressed beyond the prototype stage as the company ceased car production in 1956.

10C HRG 1½-Litre

11A: **Jaguar** XK140 Roadster was a renamed version of the XK120 of former years; with the new name came an increase in power from the famous $3\frac{1}{2}$-litre engine which had been so successful on the international sports car racing front since the war. The 3442-cc power unit developed 190 bhp at 5500 rpm (160 bhp on XK120). Also available were Drophead Coupé and Fixed-Head Coupé versions. Externally they were distinguishable from the XK120 by bolder grille bars and wrapround bumpers.

11A Jaguar XK140

11B: **Jaguar** Mark VIIM Saloon was similar to the Mark VII but with increased power output (as on the XK140) and modified front end treatment which included new wrapround bumpers, exterior mounted fog lamps, horn grilles below the headlamps, flashing trafficators and rim embellishers as standard equipment.

11B Jaguar Mark VIIM

11C: **Jenard** Jabeka Sports was designed and built by G. A. Elsmore, chief flight observer of the Westland Aircraft Co. of Yeovil, Somerset. This attractive two-seater was to be available with a choice of four power units—Supercharged Austin A40 and A50, MG $1\frac{1}{2}$-litre and Coventry Climax, but never reached the production stage—only prototypes were built.

11D: **Jensen** 541 4-Litre Sports Saloon continued with slight modifications. When first announced (in October 1953) it had an aluminium body, but by the time production started (early in 1955) a reinforced plastic version was used. The car was powered by an Austin 125 six-cylinder engine, with triple carburettors as standard.

11C Jenard Jabeka Sports

11D Jensen 541

1955

12A Kieft 1100 Sports

12A: **Kieft** 1100 Sports, an open two-seater produced by Kieft Cars Ltd of Wolverhampton under the direction of Mr Cyril Kieft, featured a Coventry Climax overhead-camshaft engine and moulded fibreglass bodywork. A Kieft was the only British car to win International Class honours on two occasions in the 1954 World's Sports Car Championship. It was available also with a 1500-cc flat-four engine with four overhead camshafts.

12B: **Lagonda** 3-Litre Saloon, a Tickford-bodied four-door model which was basically similar to the two-door saloon except that the chromium strips on the body sides were longer and the rear side windows had louvres. Also available was a Drop-head Coupé. The two-door saloon was discontinued at the end of 1954.

12B Lagonda 3-Litre

12C: **Lanchester** Sprite Mark II Saloon was a much modified and restyled version of the ill-fated Mark I which never actually reached the production stage (only three were ever built). A 1622-cc engine, which developed 60 bhp at 4200 rpm, drove through a Hobbs automatic transmission. Only ten of these were built before Lanchester ceased operations.

12C Lanchester Sprite Mark II

12D MG Magnette ZA

12D: **MG** Magnette Series ZA Saloon was continued with a modified facia. This smart four-seater featured a twin-carburettor $1\frac{1}{2}$-litre OHV engine, a full-width body with a curved radiator cowl of familiar MG form and a well-appointed interior which included pile carpets, leather upholstery and wooden facia.

13A Morgan Plus Four

13A: **Morgan** Plus Four two- and four-seater Tourer and two-seater Coupé models were continued for 1955 with minor changes and were joined by a new four-seater Coupé (shown). Powered by the 2-litre (2088-cc) Standard Vanguard engine these traditional sports cars featured a curved-back radiator with vertical chrome bars and faired-in headlamps. The two-seater Tourer was also available with the 1·9-litre (1991-cc) Triumph TR2 engine, a power unit which became standard equipment for all models in 1958.

13B: **Morris** Minor Traveller estate car was continued, together with the two- and four-door saloons and convertible versions, with a number of changes including a restyled radiator grille, modified rear light units and a revised instrument panel layout. It became one of the most popular Morris cars ever made.
13C: **Morris** Isis was introduced in February 1955 and was available as standard or de luxe Saloon or as a Traveller estate car. They were of similar appearance to the Oxford Series II but had the letters ISIS on each front wing, above the chrome flash, and featured a six-cylinder 2639-cc engine. Automatic transmission was optionally available, as an alternative to the standard four-speed manual type.

13C Morris Isis

13D: **Reliant** Regal Coupé Mark II was a modified version of the original three-wheeler first introduced late in 1951. It had a 747·5-cc engine, four-speed gearbox, box section pressed-steel chassis and hydraulic brakes. Wheelbase measured 74 in. The list price was £403.

13B Morris Minor Traveller

13D Reliant Regal Mark II

1955

14A Renault 750

14A: **Renault** 750 Saloon, Model R1062. Assembled both in its native France (designated 4CV) and also in England, using a considerable amount of British material, this rear-engined saloon was a very popular little car. It featured a 748-cc 21-bhp engine and all-independent suspension and was continued with detail modifications which included twin horn grilles on the bumper bracket, flashing trafficators and diamond-shaped badge

14B: **Riley** Pathfinder Model RMH Saloon continued into its second year of production with minor changes. Powered by a sturdy $2\frac{1}{2}$-litre 110-bhp four-cylinder engine, it featured four-light full-width bodywork with a typical Riley radiator grille.

14C: **Rolls-Royce** Silver Cloud was announced in the spring of 1955 and was virtually identical to the S-Type Bentley, except for the radiator shell design and wheel hub caps. The standard steel body had aluminium bonnet, door and boot lid panels. The 4887-cc engine—similar to the Bentley Continental power unit—had twin SU carburettors and a 6·6:1 compression ratio. As usual, the power output and torque figures were not disclosed. Automatic transmission was standard—a manual gearbox was not offered. Also available was the Silver Wraith Series E chassis. The Silver Dawn was discontinued in 1955.

14C Rolls-Royce Silver Cloud

Here is the latest, the most exciting car of a great English breed—the brilliant Riley "Pathfinder." Powered to put it in the 100 m.p.h. class with all the dash and spirit that goes with it. Styled for roomy comfort for six and with really generous luggage space. New coil spring rear suspension and torsonic front suspension, 12in. hydraulic brakes, telescopic dampers, new steering entirely free from road reaction and a host of other advanced features. *It's a new expression of a great Riley tradition.*

RILEY FOR MAGNIFICENT MOTORING

The Riley Pathfinder is fitted with Safety Glass all round.

REMEMBER—
Quality and dependability are guaranteed by the B.M.C. Used-Car Warranty and you are certain of a good deal when you sell.

BMC

RILEY MOTORS LIMITED, *Sales Division*, COWLEY, OXFORD

London Showrooms: RILEY CARS, 55-56 PALL MALL, S.W.1. Overseas Business: Nuffield Exports Ltd., Oxford and 41 Piccadilly, London, W.1

14B Riley Pathfinder

15A Rover 90

15A: **Rover** 90 Saloon continued—along with the other, similar bodied, P4 models (60 and 75)—with a number of changes including flashing trafficators as standard to replace the front-wing reflectors, vertical three-piece tail lights, a wider three-piece rear window, repositioned boot lid, larger front brakes (75 and 90) and a modified parking brake. The 75 also had a new engine—2230 cc, giving 80 bhp at 4500 rpm and the 90 engine (2638 cc, 90 bhp) had a raised compression ratio which gave it a slight increase in power output.

15B/C: **Singer** Hunter Saloon. Announced in September 1954, the medium-sized four-door Hunter model superseded the 1948–54 SM 1500 Saloon. The bodystyling was basically similar, except for the radiator grille which was of the upright 'traditional' type, sporting a horse's head mascot. The Hunter featured a modified version of the established four-cylinder 1½-litre OHC engine, fibreglass bonnet panels, twin fog lamps and a fitted tool drawer in the boot.

15D: **Standard** Ten Saloon was introduced in 1954 to fill the gap between the 2-litre Vanguard and the Eight. It was a four-light four-door saloon, powered by a 948-cc 33-bhp engine. Externally the Ten was distinguishable from the Eight by its more elaborate radiator grille. Also available was an Estate Car version with steel panelled six-light four-seater body. The latter was known as the Ten Companion (originally 'Good Companion').

15B Singer Hunter

15C Singer Hunter

15D Standard Ten

1955

16A: **Sunbeam** 90 Mark III Saloon (shown) and Drophead Coupé. These high performance $2\frac{1}{4}$-litre engined sports models were continued with a number of changes which included engine modifications—increased bhp—slotted wheel discs, laterally extended air intake grilles, air exit portholes in the scuttle sides and a redesigned facia panel. It achieved many successes in international rallies during the late '40s and the '50s. The name Talbot was dropped from the car name plates in the summer of 1954.

16B: **Sunbeam** Alpine open two-seater sports model was mechanically similar to the 90 from which it was developed, primarily for export. Externally it was distinguishable from the 90 Drophead Coupé by its flatter rear end, smaller, deeper air-intakes beside the radiator, separate sidelamps and the absence of door handles and scuttle portholes. The Alpine broke two records in Belgium on its first road test; the flying mile at 119.402 mph and the flying kilometre at 120.132 mph.

16A Sunbeam 90 Mark III

16B Sunbeam Alpine

17A: **Swallow** Doretti Sports. Attractive aluminium-and-steel-bodied two-seater built by the Swallow Coachbuilding Co. (1935) Ltd, of Walsall, Staffs and featuring the well-proved 2-litre Triumph TR2 engine mounted in a rigid chassis frame. Regrettably the model was in production for little more than one year—announced in March 1954—with initial orders being confined to the American market. Wheelbase was 7 ft 7 in, overall length 13 ft, width 5 ft 1 in.
17B/C: **Triumph** TR2 Sports continued with only minor changes, although the Convertible was joined by a Hard-top (detachable fibreglass unit) version. Powered by a 1991-cc linered-down version of the Standard Vanguard 2-litre (2088-cc) engine, this very popular sports car featured a full-width body with a squarish opening to the radiator grille.
17D: **Vauxhall** Cresta Model EIPC was a new luxury version of the Velox Saloon, added to the four-cylinder 1507-cc engined Wyvern (EIX) and the six-cylinder 2262-cc engined Velox (EIPV) which were continued with a 'new look' front end and various detail modifications. All three models featured a wide simple radiator grille incorporating the sidelamps. The Cresta was distinguished from the Velox by, among other features, white-wall tyres, chromium wheel rim embellishers, and numerous interior refinements such as leather upholstery, coat hangers and a heater as standard.
17E: **Wolseley** Six/Ninety Saloon was an addition to the Four/Forty-Four which continued unchanged; the Six/Eighty model was discontinued. The new car had a six-cylinder $2\frac{1}{2}$-litre 95-bhp power unit with twin carburettors and a full-width six-seater body, rather similar to the Four/Forty-Four but with a separate chassis, straight-through wings, less thrust forward grille, narrower tray behind the front bumper and full length base-line body flanges.

17A Swallow Doretti

17B Triumph TR2

17C Triumph TR2

17D Vauxhall Cresta

17E Wolseley Six/Ninety

1956 Many prophets of doom were forecasting that British Motor Industry exports would never be as high as they had been in 1955. Criticisms levelled at the industry included: obsolete design, poor finish, unreliability, and inefficient after-sales service and spare parts organization.

As it turned out the year was probably the toughest on record in the post-war era for British manufacturers, with a credit squeeze, a clamp down on car imports by the major markets of Australia and New Zealand, and serious labour disputes. Added to this was the rapid growth of strong foreign competition. Against this rather depressing background British manufacturers were instituting vast expansion plans—aimed not only at increasing production but also at reducing prices—and the reorganization of service and sales operations, while dismissing their critics as being over pessimistic.

On the design front the larger manufacturers were increasingly adopting tubular tyres as standard equipment, overdrive and automatic transmission systems were gaining in popularity and more and more manufacturers were offering de luxe equipment—in the form of optional extras—as a means of turning standard production cars into more luxurious models.

New models during the year tended to come from the major companies, namely the Sunbeam Rapier, the Jaguar 2.4, the Standard Vanguard Phase III and the MGA. The year's total car production was 747,922 units. Exports accounted for 335,397 cars and UK registrations for 412,525 (including hackneys).

18A AC Aceca

18A: **AC** Aceca, Hard-top Coupé alternative to the Ace open model (see 1955)—both models were continued with no material changes but the Aceca now featured front and rear bumpers. It had similar basic specifications to the Ace, except that the differential was rubber-mounted, the instrument panel was different and it was longer, wider, higher and heavier. From April 1956 both models were also available with the Bristol 2-litre engine.

18B Alvis TC108/G

18B: **Alvis** TC108/G two-door Sports Saloon featured coachwork by Graber of Berne, Switzerland. The car had a 3-litre six-cylinder 104-bhp engine, independent front suspension with wishbones and coil springs, and semi-elliptic leaf rear springs. The cleanly designed elegant body included straight-through wings, wrapround rear window and a curved bonnet, sloping down to a traditional Alvis radiator grille. The TC21-100 Grey Lady 3-Litre Saloon was discontinued in February 1956.

19A Armstrong Siddeley Sapphire 234/236

19B Armstrong Siddeley Sapphire 346

19A: **Armstrong Siddeley** Sapphire 234 and 236 Saloons. Following in the wake of the successful 3½-Litre Sapphire (renamed Sapphire 346) these two smaller models shared a completely new body and chassis but had different engines—four-cylinder, 2290-cc (234) and six-cylinder, 2309-cc (236)—plus various other differences. The body featured deep windows and a bonnet line that sloped sharply down to a traditional type radiator grille.
19B: **Armstrong Siddeley** Sapphire 346 Estate Car was a rare model based on the Mark II Limousine chassis. This impressive vehicle had an overall length of 17 ft 8 in and 11 ft 1 in wheelbase.

19C: **Aston Martin** DB2-4 Mark II Sports Saloon was facelifted for 1955 and was distinguished from the Mark I by the different rear wing line incorporating modified lighting and signalling units, a front-hinged bonnet which no longer included the side panels, and chrome side strips. Also available were drophead coupé and hard-top versions. These two were discontinued in the autumn of 1956.

19C Aston Martin DB2-4 Mark II

19D: **Aston Martin** DB3S Competition model, which, from May 1956, was available to special order with fixed-head coupé bodywork. It featured curving wings and fluting on the side of the bonnet nose above the mesh grille. The 3-litre engine developed 210 bhp at 6000 rpm.

19D Aston Martin DB3S

20A Austin A50 Cambridge

20C Austin A135

20D Bentley S-Series

20B Austin A105

20A: **Austin** A50 (Model HS5) Cambridge Saloon continued with the addition of amber flashing trafficators. This four-door model had the same body shell as the A40 (Model GS5) Saloon (*see* 1955) but with a four-cylinder 1489-cc engine and different gearbox ratios. Also offered was a Countryman (Model HP5) estate car version, to special order only.
20B: **Austin** A105 (Model BS5) Saloon. Introduced in the spring of 1956 this six-cylinder 2639-cc twin-carburettor engined model had the same basic body as the A90 Westminster (*see* 1955).
20C: **Austin** A135 four-light Touring Limousine Mark III version (Model DM5) was continued for 1956—identified by built-in combined sidelamps and flashing trafficators on the wings above the front bumper. The engine was a 3993-cc OHV Six. Also available were a Saloon (DS5) and a long-wheelbase Saloon (DS6) and Limousine (DM4).

20D: **Bentley** S-Series Saloon. Introduced in the spring of 1955 this elegant model featured a 4887-cc (95 × 114 mm) engine with a six-port cylinder head a new all-metal lightweight body and automatic transmission as standard. Wheelbase was 10 ft 3 in. Power steering and a refrigeration unit were available at extra cost.

21A Daimler One-O-Four

21A: **Daimler** One-O-Four Saloon was a $3\frac{1}{2}$-litre engined model ($4\frac{1}{2}$-litre also available) which replaced the Regency Mark II. Engine performance was greatly increased—137 bhp compared with 107 bhp on the Regency. Also available was a Lady's Model version which featured, as standard, many items found only on specialized coachbuilt models, including power-operated windows, a radio, set of suitcases and picnic case in the luggage locker, telescopic umbrella, shooting stick and vanity case.

21B: **Daimler** DK400 Limousine, a well-proportioned eight-seater which was 18 ft 1 in long, 6 ft 4 in wide and 5 ft $9\frac{3}{4}$ in high and fitted with a six-cylinder 4617-cc power unit, preselector gearbox, vacuum servo-assisted brakes and a luxurious interior.

21C: **Daimler** Conquest Drophead Coupé replaced the Conquest Roadster for 1956. It featured similar bodywork, with an occasional rear seat, and was powered by the 2433-cc 100-bhp engine. Conquest and Century Mark II $2\frac{1}{2}$-litre saloons were also available, although the former was discontinued in the summer of 1956.

21B Daimler DK400

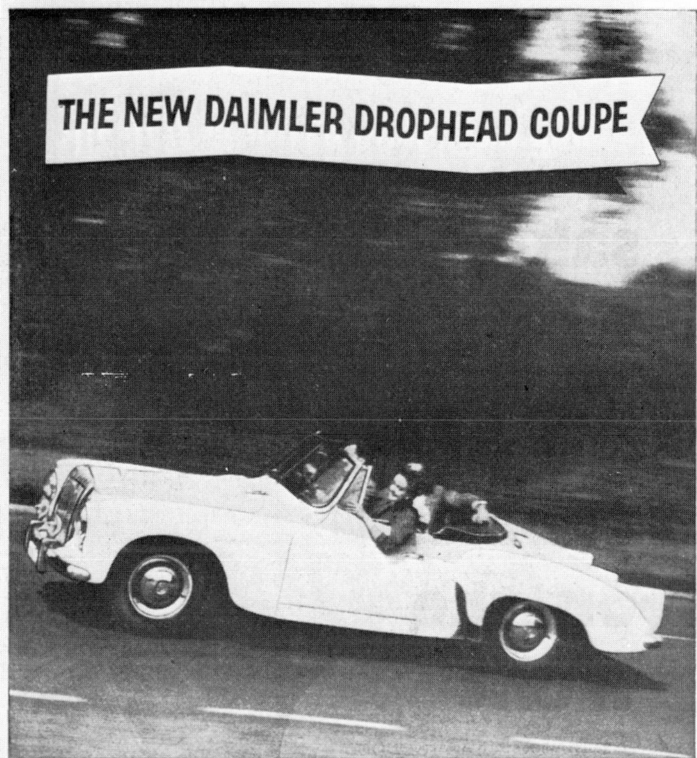

100 MPH AND ALL THIS GREATER COMFORT

- ★ *Curve-backed seats for fast-cornering comfort.*
- ★ *Transverse seat behind driver, easily detachable.*
- ★ *New washable drophead-type hood with washable lining gives maximum headroom. The flexible rear window can be zipped down.*
- ★ *Snugly-fitting wind-up windows.*
- ★ *Heating equipment as standard.*
- ★ *Higher roof and wider doors give very easy entry.*

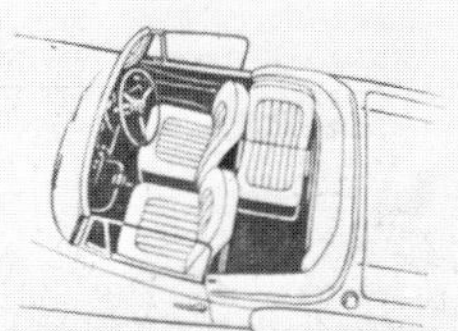

The vivid performance of the New Drophead Coupé is matched perfectly by sure, powerful braking, beautifully responsive steering and outstanding road holding. £1927.15.10 including purchase tax.

THE DAIMLER COMPANY LIMITED, RADFORD WORKS, COVENTRY

21C Daimler Conquest

22A Ford Anglia 100E

22B Ford Squire 100E

22A: **Ford** Anglia 100E Saloon was continued with detail modifications including separate amber flashing trafficators and, on the new De Luxe versions, chrome body-side strips, headlamp surrounds and window surrounds, a flat facia and improved seating. The full-width flush-sided body featured two doors and a horizontal-bar grille whereas the companion Prefect model had four doors and a vertical-bar grille. Both models were powered by the old 1172-cc 36-bhp side-valve Four engine.

22B: **Ford** Squire (shown) and Escort 100E made their début in the autumn of 1955 for the 1956 model year. Based on the Prefect and Anglia respectively, these compact little estate cars were mechanically similar to the saloons, except that a different gearbox was used and the rear suspension modified. The Squire was to the more comprehensive specification—on a par with the Prefect—and featured wooden strips on the body sides, dual windtone horns, opening (sliding) side windows and better interior finish.

22C: **Ford** Consul Mark II Saloon (*see* 23). Shown is a diesel-engined version, powered by a Perkins Four 99 engine. This model was distinguishable by the Perkins motif on the radiator grille.

22C Ford Consul 204E

23: **Ford** Consul, Zephyr and Zodiac Saloons (right to left). These new Mark II versions were introduced early in 1956 and shared a completely new full six-seater body shape although each version had its own distinctive radiator grille and styling features. There were numerous mechanical modifications including increased engine performance and revised suspension and brakes. The cheaper and least powerful of the three—the Consul 204E—had a 1703-cc four-cylinder engine whereas the Zephyr and Zodiac 206E had 2553-cc six-cylinder engines. The Zodiac was the more expensive version and included additional trim and fittings. Note the high roof line; this was changed in 1959 ('low-line models').

23 Ford Zodiac, Zephyr and Consul

1956

24A Frazer-Nash Le Mans

24A: **Frazer-Nash** Le Mans Coupé. Powered by the 1971-cc engine with a 9·0:1 compression ratio and an output of 140 bhp at 5750 rpm this two-door two-seater—first introduced late in 1953—had similar general lines to the Sebring (*see* 1955). All Frazer-Nashes were hand-built and very much tailored to meet individual owner's requirements.

24B: **Hillman** Minx Mark VIIIA De Luxe Saloon with new 'Gay Look' two-tone finish, body chrome strip and full-width tapered fairing housing the rear number plate. Convertible, Californian and Estate Car versions were also available with 'Gay Look' features. Both the Special Saloon and the Estate Car were now also powered by the OHV engine (*see* 10A) Standard (single-colour) models retained the designation Mark VIII.
24C: **Hillman** Minx Series I models were introduced in the spring of 1956 and featured new bodystyling—raised wing line, sloping bonnet and wrapround rear window—a longer and narrower radiator grille and a modified instrument panel and improved interior. Special Saloon, De Luxe Saloon and Convertible (shown) models were available. The Minx Estate Car was continued in its Mark VIII form, until May 1957.
24D: **Humber** Hawk Estate Car. Mechanically identical to the Hawk Mark VI Saloon this smart six-seater four-door model featured rear seats that could be folded down to give a spacious luggage platform—articles up to 7 ft long could be carried with the rear door panel let down to the platform position. It was introduced in October of the previous year. In April 1956 a De Luxe version of the Saloon made its appearance, designated Hawk Mark VIA.

24B Hillman Minx Mark VIIIA

24C Hillman Minx Series I

24D Humber Hawk Mark VI

25A Jaguar 2·4-Litre

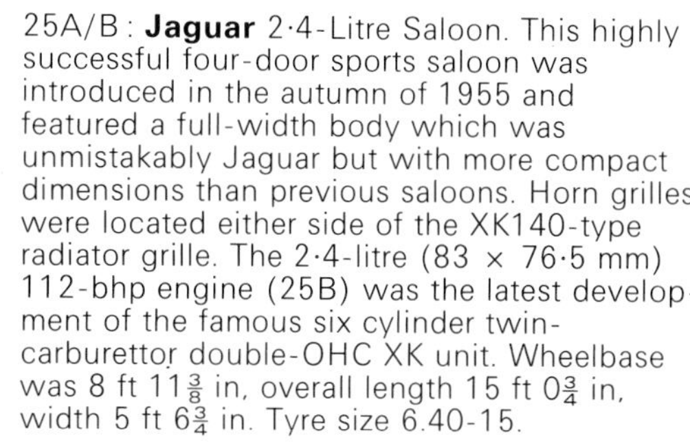
25B Jaguar 2·4-Litre

25A/B: **Jaguar** 2·4-Litre Saloon. This highly successful four-door sports saloon was introduced in the autumn of 1955 and featured a full-width body which was unmistakably Jaguar but with more compact dimensions than previous saloons. Horn grilles were located either side of the XK140-type radiator grille. The 2·4-litre (83 × 76·5 mm) 112-bhp engine (25B) was the latest development of the famous six cylinder twin-carburettor double-OHC XK unit. Wheelbase was 8 ft 11$\frac{3}{8}$ in, overall length 15 ft 0$\frac{3}{4}$ in, width 5 ft 6$\frac{3}{4}$ in. Tyre size 6.40-15.

25C/D: **Jaguar** D-Type. Immortal 3$\frac{1}{2}$-litre engined competition sports car, originally designed for the 1954 Le Mans 24-hour race—it came second to a much-larger-engined 4$\frac{1}{2}$-litre Ferrari, went one better in the ill-fated 1955 race when it came first (Hawthorn and Bueb driving) only to repeat the triumph (Sanderson and Flockhart driving) the following year. Shown are a typical D-type of the period—25C—and a part-assembled model passing along a production line—25D. Limited numbers were sold to the public.

25C Jaguar D-Type

25D Jaguar D-Type

1956

26A: **Land-Rover** Series I Regular 86 in its standard form with canvas tilt, as produced during 1953–56. It was available also with hard-top. Station Wagons were supplied on this Regular 86 chassis, (from 1954), as well as on the 107-in long-wheelbase chassis (from 1955), the latter model featuring two doors on each side and ten seats. In June 1956 the 86-in wheelbase Regular models received modifications to front wings and bonnet, and their wheelbase was increased to 88 inches.

26B: **MG** Model MGA Sports was a direct development of the prototype known as the EX182 which did so well in the 1955 Le Mans 24-hour race. This new two-seater was a complete breakaway from the traditional MG sports cars and featured a full-width body with sloping bonnet and grille, air outlet grilles on top of the scuttle and separately-styled rear wings. The 1489-cc four-cylinder engine had an 8·3:1 compression ratio and an output of 68 bhp at 5500 rpm.

26B MG MGA

26A Land-Rover Series I Regular 86

26C Morgan Four-Four Series II

26C: **Morgan** Four-Four Series II Tourer. This new lower-priced two-seater sported a body similar to the Plus Four but had a flat-back panel with a protruding petrol filler cap next to the semi- recessed spare wheel. Power came from a Ford 1172-cc four-cylinder engine which developed 36 bhp at 4400 rpm.

27A: **Paramount** $1\frac{1}{2}$-Litre Sports. Successor to the Ten Roadster (from 1950) this model—available with Tourer and Sports Saloon body styles—was powered by a 1508-cc 47-bhp engine with three-speed gearbox and featured light-alloy four-seater bodywork. Paramount Cars (Leighton Buzzard) Ltd continued small-scale production, but demand dwindled and soon the entire stock was taken over by Welbeck Motors Ltd of London who sold off the remaining cars at something like £220 less than the original list price.

27B: **Rolls-Royce** Silver Wraith continued with a larger engine—4887 cc *v.* 4566 cc—anti-roll bar at front, and automatic transmission as standard. Shown is a seven-passenger Limousine, bodied by H. J. Mulliner (Design No. 7358).

27A Paramount $1\frac{1}{2}$-Litre Sports

27C/D: **Rover** T3 Coupé, a revolutionary experimental car powered by a gas-turbine. The 110-bhp power unit was mounted at the rear and developed from an industrial gas-turbine engine (1S/60). The glass-reinforced plastic body had a low bonnet line with a deep wrapround windscreen and large rear window. The T3 also had four-wheel drive—a desirable safety factor on a car that had such a high torque to weight ratio.

27B Rolls-Royce Silver Wraith

27C Rover T3

27D Rover T3

1956

28A Singer Hunter

28A: **Singer** Hunter Saloon De Luxe as produced during March–August 1956 featured a wooden facia, spring-loaded boot lid and other refinements. Also offered (from September 1955) was an economy version, designated Hunter S, which had a painted radiator grille without the horse's head mascot and no fog lamps, chrome strips or arm rests. The specimen shown is still in daily use by a Reigate, Surrey, family and has clocked up over 100,000 miles with no major repair work except to the bodywork. Of the 3000-odd Hunters made, very few have survived.

28B: **Singer** Hunter 75 was a more powerful version, equipped with a twin overhead-camshaft version of the 1497-cc engine, producing 75 bhp at 5250 rpm. It first appeared in October 1955 and had twin Solex downdraught carburettors, 8·0:1 compression ratio, stronger clutch, divided propeller shaft and larger brakes. The front seats could be adjusted for height and tilt as well as fore-and-aft movement. Few were made, however, and the Hunter range was discontinued in the summer of 1956, shortly after Singer Motors Ltd were absorbed into the Rootes Group.

28C: **Standard** Super Ten. Introduced in the autumn of 1955 this was a better equipped version of the basic Ten (see 15D). A Super Eight and a Family Ten (early in 1956) were also introduced.

28B Singer Hunter 75

28C Standard Super Ten

29A: **Standard** Ten Companion. Based on the Super Ten this estate car variant had four side doors and double rear doors. The front seats were separately adjustable, while the rear bench seat could be folded forward to give a flat load carrying space. Maximum carrying capacity was 448 lb.

29B: **Standard** Vanguard Phase III Saloon. Entirely new except for engine and gearbox this four-light model featured a lower, longer and lighter body which was integral with the chassis, a curved single-piece windscreen and wrap-round rear window. The 2088-cc engine produced 68 bhp.

29C: **Sunbeam** Rapier Series I Hard-top Saloon. This entirely new two-door model was quite unlike any previous Sunbeams with its very modern full-width bodywork incorporating a wide and distinctive radiator grille. The car had a 1390-cc 62-bhp (gross) engine, four-speed gearbox with Laycock overdrive and two-colour body finish, all as standard. Shown is the first Rapier to be shipped to Northern Ireland.

29B Standard Vanguard Phase III

29A Standard Ten Companion

29C Sunbeam Rapier Series I

1956

30A Triumph TR3

30B Turner 803

30A: **Triumph** TR3 Sports. More powerful successor to the 1953–55 TR2 this popular version had larger twin carburettors which increased the power output from 90 to 95 bhp; it was later increased to 100 bhp, following cylinder head modifications. Externally it was distinguishable from the TR2 by a honeycomb grille over the air intake, and scuttle vents. An occasional rear seat was available.

30B: **Turner** 803 Sports. Following successes with a number of sports/. racing and competition models, Turner Sports Cars (Wolverhampton) Ltd put this two-seater into small-scale production towards the end of 1955. It was fitted with Austin A30 engine, gearbox, rear axle and front suspension, and featured a smooth, flush-sided open body made of fibreglass, with inner steel panels. Its economical engine and light bodywork resulted in very good fuel consumption figures.

30C: **Wolseley** Fifteen-Fifty Saloon. Replacement for the Four Forty-Four, this four-cylinder $1\frac{1}{2}$-litre-engined model featured a body very similar to that of the MG Magnette, which sold for the same price, although one was easily distinguished from the other, mainly by the traditional radiator grilles and different rear windows. The Fifteen-Fifty was introduced in June 1956. The six-cylinder-engined Six-Ninety Saloon was continued with minor changes and was now available with overdrive.

30C Wolseley Fifteen-Fifty

1957 After the gloomy forecasts of the previous year by so many people, it must have been with more than a little satisfaction that the British Motor Industry was able to announce that during the year they had exported more cars than in any previous comparable period. Home sales on the other hand showed an increase of only 6% over the previous year—due largely to purchase tax and credit restrictions. The year's total car export figure was 424,320, whereas UK home registrations numbered 438,301 (including hackneys); a grand total of 862,621 cars.

In addition the industry regained from Germany, during June and July, the position as leaders in the imported car market in the USA, and reduced Germany's ascendency over Britain in car exports from 27,500 in January–March to a mere 32 cars in May–July! Newcomers to car showrooms during the year included the Berkeley sports car, the Jaguar 3.4 and Mk VIII, the Singer Gazelle, the Vauxhall Victor and the Wolseley 1500 saloons.

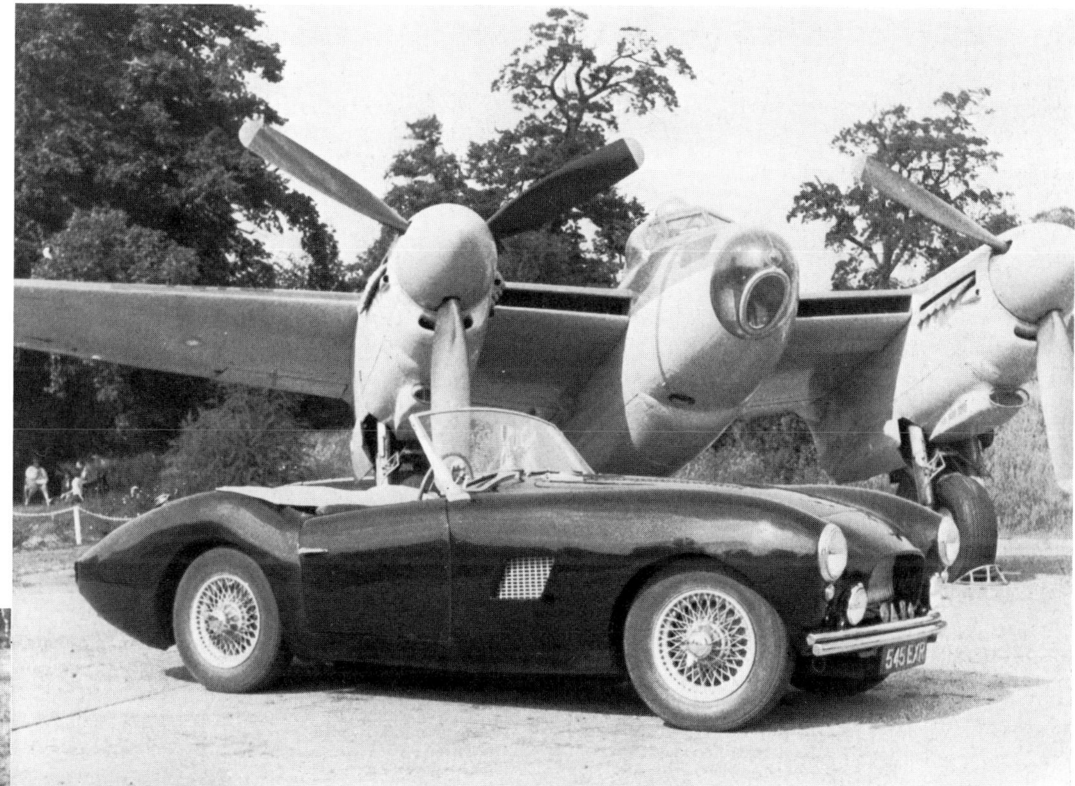

31A Allard Palm Beach

31B Allard J3R

31A: **Allard** Palm Beach Mark II 72XK Sports. This model had the same wheelbase and track as the Mark I but featured an entirely new two-seat aluminium-panelled body and either 3442-cc 190-bhp Jaguar or the new 2553-cc 90-bhp Ford Zephyr Zodiac engine. The traditional Allard divided-front-axle design was dropped in favour of an unusual system of lower wishbone and upper sliding bush, combined with laminated torsion bars.

31B: **Allard** J3R. Intended primarily for competition work this V-8-cylinder 5420-cc engined two-seater model—with alternative American engines to choice—featured a lightweight aluminium body which conformed to International Sports Car Regulations. Wheelbase was 8 ft.

1957

32A Austin A35

32A: **Austin** A35 Saloon was an uprated successor to the popular A30, powered by a 948-cc 34-bhp engine —achieved by increasing the cylinder bore size and the compression ratio—and was distinguished from the A30 by a larger rear window, heavy chrome surround to the radiator grille and flashing traffi-cators. Available in standard and de luxe Saloon, and Countryman.

32C Austin A95 Westminster

32B: **Austin** A55 Cambridge Saloon, Model HS6, replaced the A50 (HS5) early in December 1956. Differences included a more pronounced chrome radiator grille surround, chrome headlamp cowls, curved chrome flash on body sides, extended rear wing-line (length increased by some 4 in), larger boot and larger rear window. A higher compression ratio, smaller wheels and the availability of either overdrive or a Manumatic clutch had been previously introduced on the A50 in the autumn of 1956. The A40 Cambridge (GS5) was dropped.

32B Austin A55 Cambridge

32D Austin A135 Princess

32C: **Austin** A95 Westminster was the 1957 replacement for the 1954–56 A90. Available with Saloon (BS6) and Countryman estate car (BW6, shown) bodywork, it had more engine power (92 *v.* 85 bhp), a slightly longer wheelbase and a restyled body which included modified frontal treatment, a larger rear window, bodyside flashes and a squared-off rear wing line. Automatic transmission was available.

32D: **Austin** A135 Princess Mark IV Models DS7 and DM7 Saloon (shown) and Limousine featured a new steel-and-alloy streamlined Vanden Plas body on a new X-braced chassis frame, power-steering, vacuum-servo brakes and automatic transmission as standard. The six-cylinder 3·9-litre engine had twin carburettors and developed 150 bhp at 4100 rpm. From August 1957 known as *Princess*.

32E: **Austin** Model FL1 Hire Car was in production from 1948/49 and from November 1954 was available with a diesel engine (Model FL1D). It was a modification of the contemporary Model FX3 Taxi (and FX3D diesel from August 1954). All had 9 ft 2⅝ in wheelbase, Girling mechanical brakes and four fitted Smith hydraulic jacks. In 1959 they were replaced by restyled models (*q.v.*)

32E Austin Hire Car

33A Austin-Healey 100 Six

33B Bentley S-Series

33C Berkeley Sports

33A: **Austin-Healey** 100 Six (Model BN4) Sports Tourer was a new model, introduced in August 1956 and powered by a 2639-cc six-cylinder twin-carburettor engine which developed 102 bhp at 4600 rpm. The revised—longer—body featured occasional rear seats for children, resulting in rather less luggage space, a wide mesh radiator grille, bonnet top air vent, a fixed windscreen and a semi-rigid tonneau cover, designed to protect the rear seats when not in use. The four-cylinder 100 model was discontinued in late 1956. During 1958–59 the 100 Six was produced also by the MG Car Co.

33B: **Bentley** S-Series Saloon. Shown is a two-door model, bodied by James Young of Bromley, and constructed from steel and light-alloy with aluminium panelling. The Continental chassis were continued with a number of mechanical changes including increased engine power—larger carburettors and inlet valves, and a raised compression ratio.

33C: **Berkeley** Sports. Launched following countrywide publicity, this ingenious front-wheel drive miniature sports car featured body and main chassis components moulded in fibreglass, strengthened with light alloy sheet, a two-cylinder two-stroke air-cooled Anzani 322-cc engine and a three-speed gearbox. The engine was later superseded by a two-cylinder 328-cc Excelsior unit. Although basically a two-seater, it had a detachable panel which concealed space for two small children or extra luggage behind the front seats. A detachable hard-top was optionally available. The Berkeley was built by an established caravan manufacturer.

34A Ford Consul/Farnham

34A: **Ford** Consul (shown) and Zephyr Mark II Farnham Estate Cars were conversions of the respective saloon models by E. D. Abbott Ltd of Farnham, which involved extending the roof line horizontally and fitting two additional side windows and a curved window in a single rear door. Other Zephyr and Consul models were continued without material changes. Automatic transmission became optionally available on the Zephyr and Zephyr Zodiac.
34B: **Frazer-Nash** Continental Gran Turismo Coupé. Introduced in the autumn of 1956 (chassis), this powerful two-seater featured a low purposeful-looking body (introduced 1957), and was powered, initially, by a BMW 2430-cc V8 engine; a 2580 cc unit became standard later in 1957. Alternative bodies were available.

34B Frazer-Nash Continental

34C Hillman Minx Series I

34C: **Hillman** Minx Series I Estate Car, a steel-bodied, four-door model, introduced in June 1957 and similar to the Minx Series I Saloon, both mechanically and with regard to its front end styling. Wheelbase was 8 ft. The other Minx models had featured this styling from mid-1956 and were continued without material changes. All had a 1390-cc 'square' (76·2 × 76·2 mm bore and stroke) OHV Four engine.
34D: **Humber** Hawk Saloon, Series I version, was introduced in the spring of 1957. It featured a completely new low and flush-sided body with a wide radiator grille, cowled headlamps, a large boot and a wrap-round windscreen and rear window. The four-cylinder 2267-cc engine developed 73 bhp (net) at 4400 rpm. A Touring Limousine was also available. Initially the Hawk Series I models were called 'New Hawk', although this name never appeared on the cars.

34D Humber Hawk Series I

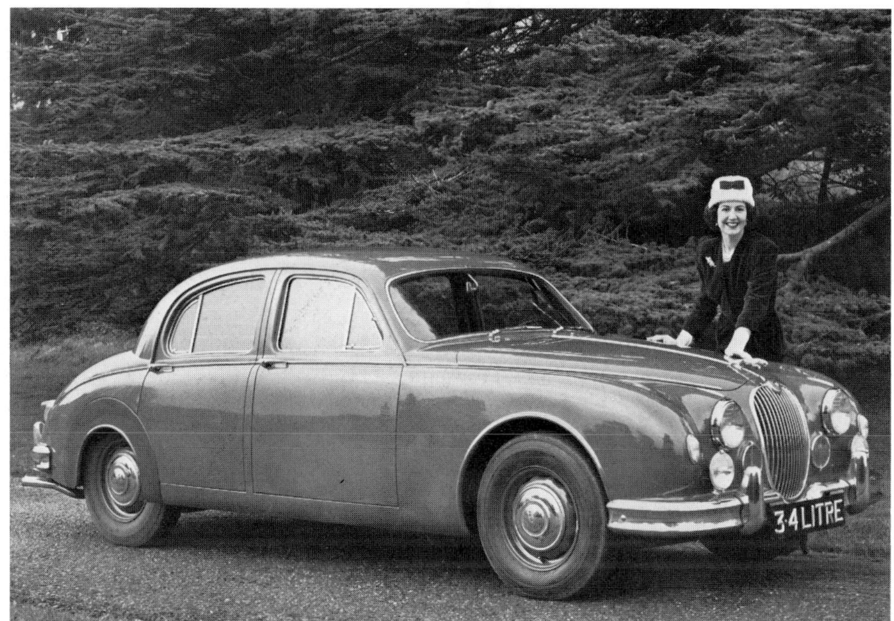

35A Jaguar 3·4-Litre

35A: **Jaguar** 3·4-Litre Saloon, introduced in January 1957, was of similar appearance to the existing '2·4' model (see page 25) but had a wider radiator grille (which was later to appear on the '2·4' also) and cut-away rear wheel covers. The twin-carburettor six-cylinder 3442-cc overhead camshaft engine developed 210 bhp at 5500 rpm. Bore and stroke were 83 × 106 mm. Twin exhaust tail pipes distinguished the '3·4' from the smaller-engined model at the rear. Overdrive or automatic transmission were available at extra cost. The car had a maximum speed of 120 mph and a fuel consumption range of 18–27 mpg. Dunlop disc brakes and wire spoke wheels were offered as optional extras from October. In late 1959 a revised model was launched, designated Series 2.

35B: **Jaguar** XK150 Drophead Coupé appeared in May 1957. Wider and roomier bodied than the preceding XK140 (1954–57) and XK120 (1948–54) this even more powerful model featured a wider radiator grille with more slats, a one-piece curved windscreen, a straightened wing line, revised instrumentation, a wider interior and higher door handles. Servo-assisted disc brakes were optionally available. The twin-OHC 3·4-litre (83 × 106 mm) engine produced 210 bhp at 5500 rpm. The XK150 was available also as a Fixed-Head Coupé and, from 1958, as a Roadster (see 49D). From October 1959 all models could be supplied with the 3·8-litre (87 × 106 mm) engine, at extra cost. In 1961 all models were discontinued and superseded by the entirely new E-Type Open Two-seater and Fixed-Head Coupé, both with 3·8-litre engine and 8 ft (*v.* 8 ft 6 in) wheelbase.

35B Jaguar XK150

36A Jaguar Mark VIII

36A: **Jaguar** Mark VIII Saloon succeeded the Mark VIIM, which it resembled apart from the following features: one-piece windscreen, two-tone paint finish divided by chrome beading, radiator grille with wider chrome surround and twin exhausts. The 3·4-litre engine had a new cylinder head, induction system and carburettors. The Mark VIIM continued to be available to special order.

36B: **Jaguar** XK SS (Super Sports). Race-bred fully road-equipped version of the highly successful D-type. Its life span was shortened as a result of a fire that destroyed part of the Jaguar factory and with it twelve completed cars and all the jigs and tools. Of the small number produced, most were exported.

36B Jaguar XK SS

36D Lotus Eleven Club

36C Lagonda Series II

36C: **Lagonda** Series II Saloon. Detail changes were made on this all-independently sprung four-door luxury model, including small mechanical modifications and the addition of a number of coachwork items. Production was discontinued in January 1958—final chassis No. LB.290/1/267.

36D: **Lotus** Eleven Club, a low streamlined sports/racing two-seater from the highly promising and already very successful Colin Chapman stable. The car featured a 1098-cc Coventry Climax engine. An Eleven Le Mans—also fitted with the Coventry Climax engine—won the 1100-cc class in the 1956 Le Mans 24-hour race.

37A: **Metropolitan** 1500. After selling so well in the United States and Canada for over three years this colourful little car became available on the British home market as Hard-top (Model HE6) and Convertible (Model HD6; shown). The Metropolitan was originally designed by Nash in the USA and from 1954 was built in Britain by Austin in conjunction with Fisher & Ludlow. Early models had a 1200-cc Austin engine. During 1954–56 it earned over 35 million dollars and for some time it was the best-selling British-built car in the USA.

37B: **MG** MGA Hard-top Coupé was an addition to the popular open model which continued with slight modifications to the hood in the form of added quarter lights; a detachable hard-top was optionally available. The output of the 1489-cc engine was increased from 68 to 72 bhp.

37A Metropolitan 1500

37C: **MG** Magnette ZB Saloon replaced the ZA model which was discontinued in the summer of 1956. Modifications included a straight chrome strip on the body sides and a parcel shelf below the facia. Manumatic two-pedal control was optional and a new variant was introduced, called the Magnette Varitone, with wrapround rear window and two-colour paint finish, divided by a chrome strip. An example of the latter is shown.

37B MG MGA

37C MG Magnette ZB

1957

38A Morris Minor 1000

38C Morris Oxford Series III

38A: **Morris** Minor 1000 Saloon. Replacement for the 1948–56 Minor Saloon, this more powerful version featured a 948-cc 37-bhp engine, close-ratio gearbox with sports type remote-control change, and a higher rear axle ratio. The appearance was changed by the introduction of a large one-piece curved windscreen and matching rear window, and the interior improved by the fitting of lidded facia glove boxes and a deeply dished steering wheel.
38B: **Morris** Cowley 1500 Saloon was uprated by the adoption of the 1489-cc 55-bhp B-Series Oxford engine. It was distinguished from the preceding 1200 version by restyled bonnet and rear wings, redesigned facia and a dished steering wheel, but remained slightly less well equipped and thus cheaper than the Oxford, which was similar in overall dimensions.

38C: **Morris** Oxford Series III Saloon featured revised body lines and fittings, modified interior and increased engine power as a result of raising the compression ratio from 7·15 to 8·3:1. Manumatic two-pedal control was available on the Saloon but not on the Traveller estate car.
38D: **Morris** Isis Series II Saloon. Top of the Morris range this six-cylinder car featured among its list of modifications a restyled bonnet with curved fluting—as on the Cowley and Oxford—restyled rear wings and lights, a mesh grille, added brightwork, revised interior and a floor-mounted gear-change. Automatic transmission was optional. A Traveller version with 65 cubic feet of luggage space was also offered. The Saloon was discontinued early in 1958, the Traveller in September 1957.

38B Morris Cowley 1500

38D Morris Isis Series II

39A Reliant Regal Mark III

39A: **Reliant** Regal Mark III four-seater three-wheeler differed from the firm's Regal Mark II by a restyled (fibreglass) body which was longer and wider, with a higher waistline and wider doors. It also had rounded front wings with a lower bonnet and an oval grille, and flush stream-lined rear wings. Wheelbase was 6 ft 2 in. A Drophead Coupé was also available. The engine was a 747·5-cc 16-bhp side-valve Four.

39B Rover 105S

39B: **Rover** 105S (shown) and 105R Saloons were additions to the P4 range and featured a twin-carb version of the 2638-cc '90' engine. The 105R had Roverdrive automatic transmission with built-in automatic overdrive; the 105S had a synchromesh gearbox with automatic overdrive. The body was as on the 75 model with bench seats; De Luxe versions had bucket seats. The 60, 75 and 90 P4 models were continued with a number of modifi-cations including extended front wings with flashing trafficator at the tip.

39C Singer Gazelle Series I

39C: **Singer** Gazelle Saloon. Following the take-over of the Singer company by the Rootes Group, production of this new four-door model (Series I) got underway late in 1956. Based on the Hillman Minx it featured an oval radiator grille and distinc-tive colour schemes to distinguish it externally, and walnut veneer and leather upholstery to give interior distinction. The car featured a raised com-pression ratio version of the 1497-cc Singer engine. A two-door Convertible model was also available.

1957

40A Standard Eight Gold Star

40A: **Standard** Eight Gold Star Saloon featured a shaped mesh radiator grille, raised compression ratio (8·25:1), external luggage boot opening and improved interior trim. The Super Saloon and Family Saloon Phase II were both discontinued. A Ten Gold Star Saloon likewise replaced the Ten Family Saloon and the Ten Companion; the Family Companion Estate Car was also discontinued.
40B: **Standard** Sportsman Saloon was externally distinguished from the Vanguard Phase III Saloon by two-colour paintwork as standard, an oblong radiator grille of vertical bars with a thick bar in the centre, dual sidelights with flashing trafficators below and additional brightwork. The twin-carburettor high-compression version of the 2088-cc engine developed 90 bhp at 4500 rpm. Overdrive was standard.
40C: **Standard** Vanguard Phase III Estate Car had similar frontal appearance to the Phase III Saloon but with a longer body and upper and lower tailgates. Wheelbase was 8 ft 6 in. De Luxe versions of both were also introduced—late in 1956—with hooded headlamps, chrome body side mouldings and bigger brakes.

40B Standard Sportsman

40C Standard Vanguard Phase III

40D Triumph TR3

40D: **Triumph** TR3 Sports two-seater, beautifully preserved and presented by its second owner at the July 1974 Ardingly, Sussex, Historic Transport Rally. Note the twin 'aero screens' and the luggage rack.

41A: **Turner** 950 Sports was a larger-engined replacement for the 803 model (see 1956). Its 948-cc Austin A35 power unit developed 34 bhp (40 bhp on later versions). Other improvements included hydraulic rear brakes, hydraulically operated clutch and the addition of an ammeter and a water temperature gauge. The car was claimed to be good for 45–50 mpg and 90 mph.

FOR THE ENTHUSIAST WITH LIMITED BUDGET
ACCLAIMED THE BEST IN THE SMALL SPORTS CAR RANGE
ALL REPLACEABLE PARTS–AUSTIN A35
PENDEFORD AIRPORT, WOLVERHAMPTON

Tel.: Ford Houses 3223

41A Turner 950 Sports

41B: **Unicar** Saloon was a plastics-based rear-engined ultra-light economy car introduced by S. E. Opperman Ltd of Boreham Wood, Herts, in the autumn of 1956. It featured a two-door body with seating for two adults and two children, an Anzani 322-cc twin-cylinder two-stroke engine, and a three-speed gearbox. The car was only 9 ft 6 in long and sold at just under £400.

41B Unicar

41C: **Vauxhall** Victor Saloon, Series F, was introduced early in 1957 to replace the Wyvern Series EIX. Prototypes had been built since 1953. The Victor was available in two versions (Standard, Model FS, and Super, Model FD) and featured a completely new body with panoramic windscreen, vertical windscreen pillars, wrapround rear window, rectangular mesh radiator grille and traditional Vauxhall flutes along the sides. The 1507-cc four-cylinder power unit developed 54·8 bhp at 4200 rpm. Wheelbase was 8 ft 2 in. Hooded headlamp rims were added in the summer of 1957.

SALUTE THE VICTOR
THE NEW VAUXHALL
The most exciting motoring news for years !
Salute the Victor, newest of the Vauxhalls . . . the family four-seater that gives motorists what they *really want!* Rarely has a new car (and the Victor is new from the ground up) aroused such excitement, such enthusiasm.
At home, and in critical overseas markets, Press and public alike are applauding. " Greatest challenge since the war in its price and size range . . ." " The car's stability and steering response are phenomenal . . ." " Will undoubtedly be among the best sellers . . ." " A world beater . . ."
To you, whether as driver or passenger, the Victor's appeal is complete and compelling! The grace of its lines encloses comfort for four large people and holiday luggage. The power of its deep-skirt 4-cylinder engine is matched by its economy in oil and petrol. First in Britain with the true panoramic windscreen, first in its class with all-synchro gears and first with features which make it a real joy to drive, for men and women alike.
See them both, the Victor (£485 plus £243 . 17 . 0 P.T.) and the Victor Super (£505 plus £253 . 17 . 0 P.T.) — at your Vauxhall dealer's today.
See them side by side with the two spacious 6-cylinder six-seater Vauxhalls, the Velox and the luxurious Cresta.

41C Vauxhall Victor Series F

42A Wolseley 1500

42B Wolseley Six-Ninety Series III

42A: **Wolseley** 1500 Saloon was a completely new model, with only the traditional radiator grille and illuminated maker's badge identifying it as a Wolseley. The neat four-door body featured two-colour paintwork and distinctive body side-flashes. The use of mechanical components common to other Nuffield models played a big part in making the price extremely attractive for a car in this class—£759 incl. tax. The $1\frac{1}{2}$-litre engine was from the Morris Oxford, but with a slightly reduced compression ratio, and the suspension system was based on that of the Morris Minor.

42B: **Wolseley** Six-Ninety Series III appeared in May 1957 and replaced the Series II version, which had only been in production for about six months. The car, which was available only in four-door Saloon form, was distinguishable from the previous version by a wider curved rear window. It also featured high-stability servo-assisted brakes. The Fifteen-Fifty was continued with minor modifications.

1958 The encouraging sales trend of the previous year was continued to the extent that total car production in 1958 topped the million mark for the first time ever. This was, in no small part, due to the substantial increase in domestic car sales, brought about by the relaxation of credit control. UK registrations, in fact, accounted for 566,319 (including 4,986 hackneys) of the total car production of 1,055,337. The export total of 484,034—valued at over £187 million—was achieved despite a fall in demand in Asia and some of the Commonwealth countries. New models introduced during the year included the Allard GT, Austin A40 Farina, Austin-Healey Sprite, Bristol 406E, Riley One-Point-Five, Standard Ensign and Vauxhall Velox/Cresta.

43B Alvis 3-Litre TC108/G

43A: **Allard** Gran Turismo Fixed-Head Coupé used the same chassis as the Palm Beach Mark II, except that it had a 20-gallon fuel tank. Introduced in October 1957, the new car featured streamlined two-door bodywork with the same general frontal appearance as the Palm Beach Mark II and air vents in the front wings. Standard power unit was the Jaguar 3·4 of 190 bhp, but larger and more powerful engines could be fitted, to customer's choice. Overdrive or automatic transmission were optionally available.

43A Allard Gran Turismo

43C Aston Martin DB Mark III

43B: **Alvis** 3-Litre Model TC108/G Drophead Coupé. Similar to the 3-Litre Saloon (*see* 1956) this elegant version was also styled by Carrosserie Graber of Switzerland, who also built most of those models which were for export; those sold in Britain were made entirely in England.

43C: **Aston Martin** DB Mark III Saloon featured a more powerful version of the 3-litre engine than was used on the DB2-4 Mark II (178 bhp *v.* 162 bhp), modified front end incorporating a mesh radiator grille, disc brakes on the front wheels and hydraulically-operated clutch. Overdrive was optionally available. A Coupé version was also offered.

43D: **Aston Martin** DB Mark III Coupé with special bodywork made by Bertone of Turin, Italy.

43D Aston Martin DB Mark III

44A: **Austin** A40 'Farina' Saloon, Model A2S6, featured bodystyling by Pininfarina, the Italian stylist and coachbuilder who was engaged by the Austin Motor Company in a consultative capacity. The two-door four-seat bodywork had a roof-line that extended back in the manner of an estate car, and a drop-down tailboard below a fixed rear window. Most of the mechanical parts were derived from contemporary BMC products including the 948-cc 34-bhp engine from the Austin A35. The photo was taken in the Champs Elysées in Paris and shows the Arc de Triomphe in the background.

44A Austin A40

44C: **Austin** Gipsy multi-purpose vehicle was developed during 1956–57 and made its public début in February of 1958. In addition to four-wheel drive it featured all-independent trailing arm suspension with Flexitor rubber springing. Engine options were 2·2-litre four-cylinder petrol or diesel, with four-speed gearbox and two-speed auxiliary gear.

44B Austin A105 Vanden Plas

44B: **Austin** A105 Vanden Plas Saloon, Model BS8, was a luxury version of the standard A105 and appeared in the spring of 1958. Overdrive was fitted as standard; automatic transmission was optional. The basic Model BS7 was continued without material changes. It was an Austin A105 that won the 1957 British Mobilgas Economy Run, averaging 33·60 mpg over a difficult 1000-mile course. Both versions had a 102-bhp OHV Six engine.

44C Austin Gipsy

45A Austin-Healey Sprite

45A: **Austin-Healey** Sprite, Model AN5, was a highly successful little sports car which became affectionately known as the 'Frogeye', in view of its prominent headlamps. Produced from March 1958 until April 1961, it featured a smooth-countered flush-sided two-seater body—the bonnet-cum-front wing assembly was hinged just forward of the windscreen—with an oval mesh radiator grille. The reliable BMC A-Series 948-cc power unit had twin carburettors and developed 43 bhp (net) at 5000 rpm. Wheelbase was 6 ft 8 in and the overall length 11 ft $5\frac{1}{4}$ in, including front bumper.

45B: **Austin-Healey** 100 Six Sports two-seater, Model BN6, replaced the two/four-seater (BN4) version in the early part of 1958. The latter was, however, reintroduced later in the year (built by MG) and the two versions then ran concurrently until both were eventually superseded by the 3000 Model BN7 (*see* 1959). Compared with the two/four-seater the Model BN6 featured a larger boot and two 6-Volt batteries (instead of one 12-Volt unit), located at each side of the spare wheel, which was moved forward.

45B Austin-Healey 100 Six

45C Bentley Flying Spur

45C: **Bentley** Flying Spur, a six-light four-door sports saloon built by H. J. Mulliner on the Continental chassis, was similar in appearance to the two-door Continental but had a step at the rear window, instead of the sweep of the tail line. Although both cars had the same overall height, the Flying Spur had more headroom for rear seat passengers and greater luggage space.

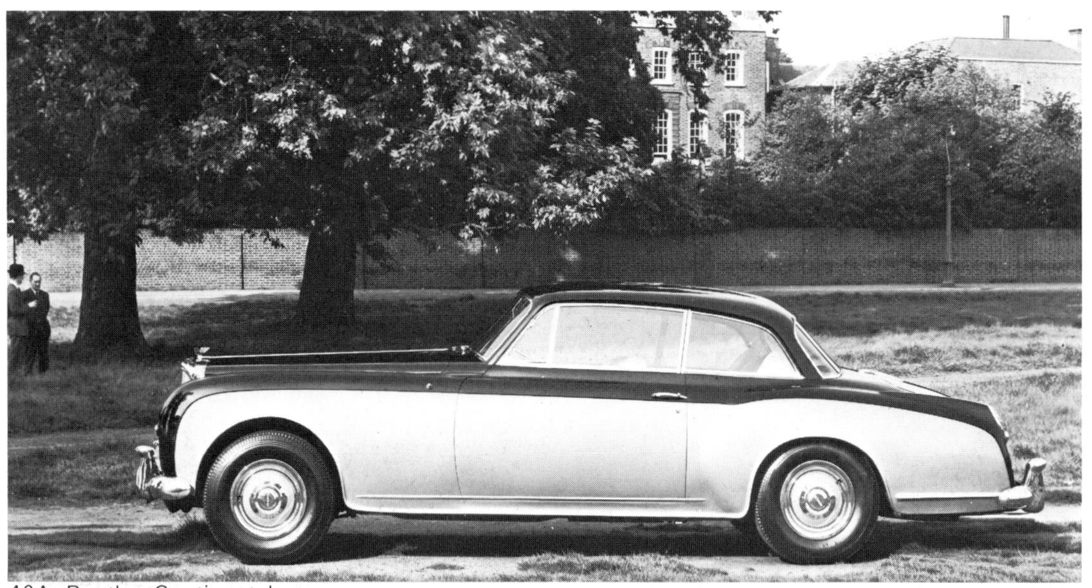

46A Bentley Continental

46A: **Bentley** Continental chassis continued without material changes. Shown is an elegant two-door model with coachwork by Park Ward & Co. The rear seat could be hinged upwards; in conjunction with a concealed valance extension this gave additional luggage space. Air conditioning was introduced as an option on all Bentley cars. The engine was a 4887-cc six-cylinder with 8·0:1 compression ratio, good for a maximum speed of 120 mph.

46B: **Berkeley** Sports. The Berkeley range was extended in the autumn of 1957 by the introduction of a new three-cylinder two-stroke 492-cc triple-carburettor engine and a new hard-top coupé body style. The '492' had the same body as the '328' and featured a four-speed gearbox. The '328' Sports was continued with a number of modifications but only up until the spring when it was discontinued (it re-appeared in 1960 with a four-speed gearbox, but not for long). The '492' Sports and Drophead Coupé models were available to either a standard or de luxe specification. All had front-wheel drive.

46B Berkeley Sports

46C Bond Minicar Mark E

46C: **Bond** Minicar Mark E two-door open three-wheeler was distinguishable from its predecessor—the Minicar Mark D De Luxe—by a new flat-sided body with straight-through wings and a wider oval radiator grille. It also featured a four-speed gearbox and a wrapround curved windscreen. The Villiers 197-cc single-cylinder two-stroke engine developed 9 bhp at 4000 rpm.

47A: **Bristol** 406E Saloon was an export-only model with bodywork by Gebr. Beutler of Switzerland. The car featured Bristol's new 2216-cc six-cylinder engine, which developed 105 bhp at 4700 rpm, and servo-assisted disc brakes. Fog lamps were fitted at each end of the wide mesh radiator grille. Wheelbase was 9 ft 6 in and overall length 16 ft.
47B: **Citroën** ID19 Saloon, a revolutionary front-wheel-drive model which was produced in its native France from late in 1956 and then also in England from early in 1958. This 'age-less' car featured a highly advanced hydro-pneumatic suspension system which kept the car at the same height and on an even keel whatever the load, camber or road surface, powered front-wheel disc brakes, a 1·9-litre four-cylinder engine and ultra-streamlined bodywork. The ID19 was a less-expensive version of the luxurious DS19, which had been introduced in France at the end of 1955.

47B Citroën ID19

47A Bristol 406E

47C Elva Mark III Sports

47C: **Elva** Mark III Sports. This limited-production competition car was built by Elva Cars of Bexhill-on-Sea, Sussex and featured a Coventry Climax 1098-cc 84-bhp engine (1½-litre version also available), an MG gearbox and a low flat body mounted on a multi-tubular space frame. Also available was the Elva Courier, which was powered by a 1½-litre MG engine.
47D: **Fairthorpe** Electron Minor Convertible, a light plastic-bodied two-seater (occasional three-seater) powered by a Standard Ten 948-cc engine with a raised compression ratio of 8·25:1. Also available from this small Buckinghamshire firm were the Electron Sports (with Coventry Climax engine) and the Atomata (with BSA 646-cc Golden Flash engine).

47D Fairthorpe Electron Minor

1958

48A Ford Anglia

48B Ford Escort

48C Ford Zephyr

48A: **Ford** Anglia Saloon, Model 100E, was continued with a number of changes which included a new mesh radiator grille, modified front lamp bezels, larger rear window and rear lamp assemblies, chromium bumpers, and a new facia layout. Newton-drive two-pedal control was optionally available for approximately one year. Saloon De Luxe featured chrome strips on body sides, chrome window surrounds and other refinements.
48B: **Ford** Escort Estate Car was derived from the Anglia 100E and continued with modifications similar to those made on the Anglia (*q.v.*). The wood mouldings which previously distinguished the more luxurious Squire Estate Car (*see* 1956) were replaced by chrome strips.
48C: **Ford** Zephyr Mark II Saloon, Model 206E, was continued with a number of modifications including a new grille of horizontal bars with rectangular combined side lights and flashing direction indicators. The luxurious Zodiac (206E) continued with modified front lights—as on the Zephyr—and detail interior improvements. The Consul (204E) range was extended by the addition of a De Luxe Saloon. Farnham Estate Cars were also available; these were conversions of the saloons.
48D: **Frisky** Sport Convertible was a very small rear-engined four-wheeled two-seater, built by Henry Meadows (Vehicles) Ltd of Wolverhampton. It featured a Michelotti styled body—with a detachable tail—and a Villiers air-cooled 342-cc 16·5-bhp engine. A closed version was also made. In October a sports roadster was announced—the Frisky Sprint—but this model did not reach the production stage.

48D Frisky Sport

49A Hillman Minx Series II

49B Hillman Husky Series I

49C Humber Hawk Series I

49D Jaguar XK150

49A: **Hillman** Minx Series II Special Saloon was distinguished from the Series I Special by a restyled mesh radiator grille, incorporating the sidelights and 'Hillman' in script. The engine was also modified. Other Minx models were the De Luxe ('Jubilee') Saloon, Convertible and Estate Car. Manumatic transmission was optional on all except the Special Saloon.
49B: **Hillman** Husky Series I Estate Car, which replaced the 1954–57 Mark I, had similar features to the Series II Minx Special Saloon and was powered by the 1390-cc overhead-valve 51-bhp engine. Wheelbase was 7 ft 2 in, overall length 12 ft $5\frac{1}{2}$ in.

49C: **Humber** Hawk Estate Car. Based on the Hawk Series I Saloon (*see* 1957) this spacious version had a load volume of 56 cu. ft with the rear seat folded down, and about half that capacity with the seat raised. The divided rear door comprised a top-hinged glazed upper half and a bottom-hinged tailgate. Mechanically, the only difference between the Saloon and Estate Car lay in the springing.
49D: **Jaguar** XK150 Roadster was introduced in the spring of 1958. This open two-seater was available—initially for export only—with a choice of three $3\frac{1}{2}$-litre engines: twin-carburettor 'standard', 190-bhp; twin-carburettor 'blue top', 210-bhp; and triple-carburettor 'gold-top', 252-bhp. When fitted with the 'gold top' engine it was called the XK150 Roadster Type S and featured other differences including a stronger clutch and special quick-changing pads for the servo-assisted disc brakes. The XK150 Roadster became available on the home market in the autumn of 1958.

1958

50A Jensen 541 R

50B: **Land-Rover** 88 and 109 Series I models were superseded early in 1958 by a new range, designated Series II. They were distinguishable by somewhat 'rounder' bodystyling with rocker panels below the doors. The 10-seater Station Wagon was continued on the earlier 107-in wheelbase Series I chassis until November. Its replacement, the 109 Series II (shown here in military guise), followed shortly afterwards. The 1952–58 1997-cc petrol engine was replaced by a 2286-cc unit. A 2052-cc diesel engine was optional.

50C: **Lotus** Elite Coupé was a highly attractive Gran Turismo two-seater which heralded Colin Chapman's graduation from special sports/racing cars into true passenger-car production. The Elite featured a 1216-cc 72-bhp Coventry-Climax engine, all-independent suspension, disc brakes all round, and resin-bonded fibreglass bodywork.

50A: **Jensen** 541R Saloon first appeared in October 1957, priced £1910 plus £956 PT. Differences from the standard and de luxe 541 versions included increased power from its Austin DS7 engine, a new slightly smaller gearbox with closer overall ratios, rack and pinion steering and disc brakes all round. Externally the R was distinguished by an outlet with plated grille in the bonnet top, torpedo-shaped mouldings above the rear wheels, and a top-hinged luggage boot lid. Top speed: over 125 mph; cruising: 90–100 mph.

50C Lotus Elite

50D: **MG** MGA Twin Cam open two-seater was externally similar to the MGA, apart from 'Twin Cam' motifs on the scuttle and boot lid, but was powered by a twin-overhead-camshaft 1588-cc engine—achieved by enlarging the bore size to 75·4 mm—which had a 9·9:1 compression ratio and developed 108 bhp (gross) at 6700 rpm, and was fitted with disc brakes all round. Centre lock disc wheels were standard. Also available was a Coupé version. The 1489-cc MGA models were continued without material changes.

50B Land-Rover Series II

50D MG MGA Twin Cam

51A Morgan Plus Four

51C Morris Oxford Traveller Series IV

51A: **Morgan** Plus-Four was continued with a number of new features which included a wider body—a total of 5 inches when measured across the seats—and a lowered radiator cowl, which resulted in a shorter grille. Wire wheels were optionally available.

51B Morris Minor 'Special'

51D Peerless Gran Turismo

51B: **Morris** Minor with a difference: a rather bizarre special-bodied version, snapped in the London SE area in the late sixties. It had a top-hinged glass-panelled tailgate allowing access to a rear-facing back seat.

51C: **Morris** Oxford Traveller Series IV all-steel bodied four-door estate car replaced the 1956–57 Series III version in the summer of 1957. Duo-tone colour schemes were optionally available. An unusual feature was the provision of two fuel filler caps, one on either side of the car, for the single 11-gallon tank. Half-ton Pickup and Van versions were also produced (1956–60).

51D: **Peerless** Gran Turismo. Two-door sports saloon with fibreglass bodywork which Peerless Motors Ltd of Slough, Bucks, put into limited production in the spring of 1958. The 1991-cc 100-bhp engine and the gearbox were Triumph TR3 units, with overdrive fitted as standard. In June 1959 it was replaced by a modified (Phase 2) version.

52A: **Riley** One-Point-Five Saloon was powered by a lively $1\frac{1}{2}$-litre twin-carburettor BMC B-Series engine which developed 68 bhp at 5400 rpm. It had the same body shell as the less powerful Wolseley 1500 (*see* 1957), but was distinguished by a traditional Riley grille and more elaborate brightwork. The typically Riley interior included a walnut facia-panel and comprehensive instrumentation. The car was competitively priced at £864.

52A Riley One-Point-Five

52C: **Rolls-Royce** Silver Cloud with rather unusual convertible coachwork by Freestone and Webb. The two-door body featured slightly concave sides, prominent rear tail fins and an enormous luggage compartment.

52B Riley Two-Point-Six

52B: **Riley** Two-Point-Six Model UA Saloon was in production during 1957–59. Although externally rather similar to the Pathfinder (*see* 1955), which was discontinued early in 1957, it was distinguished by cowled headlamps, separate sidelamps and flashing direction indicators, a wider rear window, fog lamps mounted on the front overriders and two-tone paintwork. The six-cylinder 2639-cc engine developed 101 bhp at 4750 rpm, and the car was capable of speeds in excess of 100 mph.

52C Rolls-Royce Silver Cloud

53A Singer Gazelle Series II

53A: **Singer** Gazelle Series II. The Estate Car shown was added to the Saloon and Convertible which were modified (became Series II) in the autumn of 1957. Changes included a different front end in which grilles with horizontal bar replaced the pressings on each side of the radiator grille, cowled headlamps and a bonnet motif. The capacity of the petrol tank was increased to 10 gallons and overdrive became optionally available. In the spring of 1958 a 1494-cc overhead-valve engine and recirculating ball type steering gear were introduced; the range then became known as the Series IIA.

53B Standard Pennant

53C Standard Ensign

53B: **Standard** Pennant Saloon was a more expensive supplement to Standard's small car range. It appeared longer than the other models as a result of the extended front and rear wing lines. It also featured a larger rear window, a dual colour scheme divided by a plated moulding strip and a new-style radiator grille. The 948-cc engine was retained, in modified form, and Standrive two-pedal transmission was optional.

53C: **Standard** Ensign Saloon was a cheaper version of the Vanguard III and featured the same body shell albeit distinguished by a simple mesh grille. Mechanical differences included a slightly smaller engine—1670-cc capacity—and a four-speed gearbox with central floor change lever.

1958

54A: **Sunbeam** Rapier Series II appeared early in the year and differed from the Series I by an completely changed front end and flared tail fins which merged with distinctive full-length bodyside flashes. Mechanical changes included the adoption of a 1494-cc 73-bhp engine, called the Rallymaster. A Convertible version was also offered.

54B: **Triumph** TR3A Sports Roadster differed from the preceding TR3 by a new wide and shallow radiator grille, slightly recessed headlamps, overrider upper stay-bars and external lockable handles for doors and luggage boot. A hard-top coupé was also available. The TR3A had been available for export from August 1957 and in January 1958 replaced the TR3 on the home market.

54A Sunbeam Rapier Series II

54B Triumph TR3A

54C Vauxhall Victor

54C: **Vauxhall** Victor Estate Car, Model FW, was introduced in March 1958. All Victors now had hooded headlamp rims and Newton drive two-pedal control was an optional extra.

54D: **Vauxhall** Velox Saloon, Model PAS, was fitted with a completely new and attractive American-style body which it shared with the Cresta (PAD) version and which featured a full panoramic windscreen with a slope of 45 degrees, but with a slight curvature from top to bottom to reduce reflections, a three-piece rear window, miniature rear wing fins and slightly-cowled headlamps. The six-cylinder 2262-cc engine and the gearbox were modified versions of well-tried Vauxhall units. The Cresta, which was a more luxurious version of the Velox, had additional brightwork and fittings, and white-wall tyres.

54D Vauxhall Velox

1959 It was estimated, in the autumn, that one in every three families in Great Britain owned a car. With attractively-priced new models reaching the showrooms and production figures continuing to rise rapidly, the position looked encouraging as Britain prepared to move into the sixties.

Of the year's total car production of 1,231,414, no fewer than 568,971 were exported, valued at £222,531,517; UK registrations accounted for 662,443 (including hackneys). The number of imported cars had also risen—26,998 compared with 10,940 for the previous year. Apart from anything else, 1959 was the year of the Mini. This incredible little car started its very successful run in the summer and was an immediate hit with rich and poor alike. Also new to the public were the Aston Martin DB4, the BMC $1\frac{1}{2}$-litre 'Farina' range, Bristol 406, Daimler SP250, Rover 3-Litre, Sunbeam Alpine and Triumph Herald.

55A: An assembly of most of the British car types available for purchase in the United States of America in the early part of 1959.

55A British 1959 models in New York

55B AC Ace

55B: **AC** Ace with hard-top joined the Ace open sports and Aceca models which were continued without material changes. The fibreglass hard-top was detachable. Approximately 90 per cent of AC cars were exported, mainly to the USA.

55C: **Alvis** 3-Litre TD21 Park Ward-bodied Saloon was distinguished from the TC108/G (Graber) version (*see* 1956) by a more curved bonnet top and nose, smaller one-piece rear window, number plate on the rear panel and revised frontal treatment. A Drophead Coupé version was also available. The 2993-cc engine was given a six-port cylinder head, new carburettors and a revised exhaust system early in the year.

55C Alvis 3-Litre TD21

1959

56A: **Armstrong Siddeley** Star Sapphire Six-light Saloon was similar in appearance to the Sapphire 346 (*see* 1955) except that it had cutaway rear wheel covers, doors hung on concealed hinges at the leading edges, a Sphinx mascot on the bonnet and different frontal treatment. The car featured a new 3·9-litre six-cylinder engine, automatic transmission, servo brakes (discs on the front) and power-assisted steering, all as standard equipment.

56A Armstrong Siddeley Star Sapphire

56B Aston Martin DBIII

56B: **Aston Martin** DBIII Drophead Coupé (shown) and Saloon were continued with modifications which included a hydraulic booster for the braking system and an alternative choice of—2922-cc—engine: a Special series engine with three SU carburettors or Competition engine with three Weber carburettors. A Fixed-head Coupé with the Special series engine and twin exhausts as standard was added in the late spring, but by the autumn all three versions were discontinued.

56C: **Aston Martin** DBR1/300, winner of the 1959 World Sports Car Championship. Shown is Roy Salvadori winning Le Mans; together with Shelby, as co-driver, the car covered 2701 miles. A DBRI/300 also came second. The other successes were the 1000 km Nürburgring (Moss and Fairman as drivers) and the Tourist Trophy (Moss, Shelby and Fairman).

56C Aston Martin DBR1/300

56D: **Aston Martin** DB4 Saloon was a close-coupled four-seater, styled by Carrozzeria Touring of Milan and built by Tickford in England. The impressive car had a sloping roof which merged neatly into the tail that housed a completely separate luggage boot—the first post-war Aston Martin in which the boot did not link with the passenger compartment—and a traditional Aston Martin front end. The 3·7-litre six-cylinder engine, which was a direct development from the 'Le Mans-bred' DBR2/370 unit, developed 240 bhp at 5500 rpm.

56D Aston Martin DB4

57A: **Austin** A55 Cambridge Mark II 'Farina' Saloon. This new Saloon—available in either standard or de luxe form—featured bodystyling by Pininfarina of Italy, using straight lines and finned rear wings. The well tried 1489-cc BMC B-Series engine, which was continued with a number of modifications, developed 53 bhp (gross) at 4350 rpm. A Countryman estate car version was added in the following year.
57B: **Austin** Taxi, Model FX4D, was introduced in mid-1959. It had a redesigned body, a 2·2-litre diesel engine and optional automatic transmission. The Hire Car version was designated FL2D.
57C: **Austin-Healey** 3000 Sports Roadster, Model BN7, superseded the 100 Six. It was distinguished by a '3000' flash on the horizontal slatted radiator grille and featured a larger (2912-cc) six-cylinder engine which developed 132 bhp (net) at 4750 rpm, a new front suspension system, and front disc brakes as standard. Also available was a two/four-seater (BT7) version.

57A Austin A55 Cambridge Mark II

57B Austin Taxi

57D Berkeley Foursome

57E Berkeley B95

57C Austin-Healey 3000

57D: **Berkeley** Foursome Sports. Developed from the 492-cc engined two-seater (*see* 1958), this four-seater was introduced in the autumn of 1958. It was also available with hard-top. The two-seater models were continued under the Twosome label. By March 1959, however, the complete range was discontinued and replaced by a new model (*see* 57E).
57E: **Berkeley** B95 Sports (shown) and Hard-top were powered by a Royal Enfield four-stroke two-cylinder 692-cc 40-bhp engine and externally differed from the earlier models mainly by the modified front. A B105 version, also available, had a higher performance engine (50 bhp at 6250 rpm). Larger-bodied versions (QB) were also made.

58A Bristol 406

58A: **Bristol** 406 Saloon had a completely new aerodynamically styled two-door body—built by Jones of Willesden—as well as a larger 2·2-litre 105-bhp six-cylinder engine and servo-assisted disc-brakes all round. The luxurious interior included reclining seats with hinged headrests.
58B: **Daimler** SP250 Sports two-seater was announced in the spring, initially for export only with left-hand drive (SP250 LH Dart) and represented something of change for the Daimler company. The powerful $2\frac{1}{2}$-litre V8 engine, which developed 140 bhp at 5800 rpm, made the car a particularly exciting performer. Disc brakes were standard, and overdrive or automatic transmission optional equipment. Wheelbase was 7 ft 8 in.

58B Daimler SP250

58C: **Daimler** Majestic Saloon was similar in appearance to the One-O-Four (*see* 1956) but with increased body width, a lower radiator, smoother rear wing line and detail differences. The six-cylinder 3·8-litre engine developed 147 bhp at 4400 rpm. Automatic transmission and disc brakes were standard.

58C Daimler Majestic

58D Ford Zephyr

58D: **Ford** Consul, Zephyr and Zodiac Mark II models underwent a number of styling changes early in the year, including a lower roof line, stainless steel surrounds to windscreen and rear window cappings, chrome headlamp bezels, restyled rear lamp clusters and a modified facia layout. Shown is a Zephyr Convertible.

58E: **Hillman** Minx Series III models featured a larger engine—1494-cc, 52·5 bhp (gross) at 4400 rpm—and differed externally from the Series II mainly by the revised radiator grille. Shown is the Special Saloon; also available were a De Luxe Saloon, Convertible and Estate Car. The 1390-cc Husky Series I was continued unchanged.

58E Hillman Minx Series III

59A Humber Super Snipe Series I

59C MG Magnette Mark III

59A: **Humber** Super Snipe Series I was a new car, using the same body shell as the Hawk but with a distinctive radiator grille and winged bird motif on the bonnet. It was powered by a 105-bhp 2651-cc six-cylinder engine with a new three-speed gearbox and featured servo-assisted brakes. Also available were Touring Limousine and Estate Car versions. All had 9 ft 2 in wheelbase.

59B: **Jaguar** Mark IX Saloon. Although outwardly identical to the Mark VIII, except for the rear-end motif, this car had numerous mechanical differences, including a larger six-cylinder engine—twin-carburettor, 3781 cc, 220 bhp—power assisted steering, and disc brakes all round. Automatic transmission or overdrive were optionally available.

59C: **MG** Magnette Mark III 'Farina' Saloon succeeded the Magnette ZB Saloon early in the year. As with the other BMC models in this class the body was styled by Pininfarina; it was distinguishable mainly by its traditional MG radiator grille. The $1\frac{1}{2}$-litre engine had twin carburettors and developed 66·5 bhp at 5200 rpm.

59D: **Morgan** Plus Four Drophead Coupé was continued with a number of changes which included the spare wheel recessed in the sloping tail, a rear-mounted 12-gallon fuel tank, and narrower running boards. These modifications also applied to the two-seater Tourer. The four-seater Tourer was also continued. Disc brakes became optional on all models.

59B Jaguar Mark IX

59D Morgan Plus Four

60A Morris Mini-Minor

60C Princess/Vanden Plas

60C: **Princess** Long-wheelbase 'Special Equipment' Limousine. This Vanden Plas-bodied luxury Austin model was similar to the long-wheelbase Limousine, but included as standard fitments: automatic transmission, power steering, electrically-operated division, footrests and mohair rugs in rear compartment, and an electric clock and cigar lighter for the rear-seat passengers.

60A: **Morris** Mini-Minor Saloon. This incredibly successful little car was officially announced in August 1959, although the eager motoring press had previously sampled its delights in the spring of that year. The brain child of Alec Issigonis it featured a simple but practical two-door body with a 10 in. wheel at each corner, a transversely-mounted 848-cc 34-bhp (net) engine, four-speed gearbox, front-wheel drive and all-independent rubber cone-spring suspension. Also available was an Austin version—then called the Seven—which was distinguishable by its different grille. Both versions were available in basic and de luxe forms, priced at £497 and £537 resp. (incl. PT). The Austin version's name was sometimes spelled as Se7en but before long both were universally referred to as 'Mini'.

60B: **Morris** Oxford Series V 'Farina' was identical to the Austin A55 Cambridge (*q.v.*) except for radiator grille design, detail body fittings, badges and interior layout. With detail modifications it remained in production—in Saloon and Traveller form—until 1971.

60B Morris Oxford Series V

60D: **Renault** Dauphine Saloon, Model R1090. Announced in France in the autumn of 1955 it was also assembled in the UK, at Acton, from the Summer of 1956. It was a rear-engined four-door four-seater powered by a bored-out 845-cc 30-bhp derivative of the 4CV engine and featured a unitary body-cum-chassis, three-speed gearbox and all-independent suspension. Modifications for 1959 included a raised compression ratio and a thermostatic control for the heater.

60D Renault Dauphine

61A Riley 4/Sixty-Eight

61C Rover 60

61A: **Riley** 4/Sixty-Eight Saloon was one of the new BMC 1½-litre 'Farina' range of models. It was mechanically similar to the MG Magnette Mark III (*q.v.*), but was easily distinguishable by its traditional Riley-style radiator grille.

61B: **Rolls-Royce** Silver Cloud Long-Wheelbase Saloon was a Park Ward conversion of the elegant steel saloon, lengthened to suit the 4-inch increase in wheelbase. The car was designed for dual-purpose use viz. as a limousine, chauffeur driven, with the electrically-operated glass division raised, as well as for holiday/pleasure motoring when the division could be lowered. The side windows were also electrically-operated.

61D Rover 3-Litre

61C: **Rover** 60 or Sixty (P4) Saloon was continued with detail modifications which included a modified grille and a redesigned rear number plate mounting. These changes also applied to the 75, 90 and 105 models—the 105R had been discontinued in the summer of 1958 and the 105S became known as the 105 until it was also dropped, later in 1959.

61D: **Rover** 3-Litre (P5) Saloon was the first Rover to have a unitary body-cum-chassis structure, albeit with a front sub-frame. It was noticeably longer, lower and wider than the other Rover Cars and featured a six-cylinder 2995-cc 115-bhp engine, four-speed gearbox and servo-assisted brakes. The front and rear bench seats had folding arm rests and were trimmed throughout in leather; separate front seats were optional.

61B Rolls-Royce Silver Cloud

1959

62A: **Singer** Gazelle Series III Saloon was distinguishable from the Series II version by the reshaped body side-flashes, with 'Gazelle' located on the top of each flash near the headlamps. Convertible and Estate Car versions were also available.
62B: **Standard** Ten Companion Estate Car was continued with a number of styling changes which included a grille of three horizontal bars incorporating combined sidelights and flashing trafficators, and wings which were extended to form hoods for the headlamps.
62C: **Standard** Vanguard Vignale Saloon. Although mechanically similar to its predecessor—the Vanguard Phase III—this new model featured subtle body changes made by the Italian stylist Michelotti (in conjunction with Vignale), including a higher roof line, larger windows, a new radiator grille flanked by front lights set in chrome extensions, and modified rear light clusters. The Vanguard Estate Car featured similar changes.
62D: **Sunbeam** Alpine was an attractive new two-seater high-performance open sports car, featuring a number of components developed from those of the Sunbeam Rapier, including a 1494-cc twin-carburettor 78-bhp engine and independent coil spring and wishbone front suspension. When not in use the folding hood disappeared completely into a recess behind the rear 'occasional' seat. White-wall tyres and wire spoke wheels were optional extras, as was a detachable hard-top.

62C Standard Vanguard Vignale

62A Singer Gazelle Series III

62B Standard Ten Companion

62D Sunbeam Alpine

63A Triumph Herald

63A: **Triumph** Herald Saloon. Styled by the Italian Giovanni Michelotti this highly successful car included many interesting and desirable features, such as all-independent suspension, a turning circle smaller than that of a London taxi cab, a chassis without greasing points, and an all-steel body, the front section of which was hinged at the forward end to give easy access to the engine, steering gear and front suspension. The 948-cc engine and gearbox were similar to those of the Standard Ten. Also available was a Coupé version which featured a twin-car-burettor 948-cc engine and a sloping roof line. A Convertible was launched in 1960.

63B: **TVR** Grantura Sports Coupé, was introduced onto the British market early in 1959, following a successful four-year tie-up between two Blackpool engineers, *TreVoR* Wilkinson and Bernard Williams, and an American, Ray Saidel, during which time a number of these cars—and early models—achieved successes in American sports car events. It featured fibreglass bodywork and a choice of three power-units: Coventry Climax FWE 1216-cc (as on the Lotus Elite), Ford 100E standard or Ford 100E Super-charged. In America the car was known as the Jomar.

63C: **Vauxhall** Victor Series II Saloon replaced the original edition early in the year. It was distinguishable mainly by smooth rear-door panels, full-width radiator grille with protruding oval sidelights, smooth wrapround bumpers and a reshaped bonnet. The standard model is shown.

63D: **Wolseley** 15/60 Saloon was fifth in the new BMC $1\frac{1}{2}$-litre 'Farina' range and had a traditional radiator grille with illuminated name badge, flanked by horizontal air inlets. It was basically similar to the Austin A55 (*q.v.*) and Morris Oxford Series V (*q.v.*), but not available in estate car form.

The T.V.R. GRANTURA
Elegance, Performance, Controllability
LAYTON SPORTS CARS LTD
HOO-HILL WORKS • BISPHAM ROAD • LAYTON • BLACKPOOL
Tel.: 27676

63B TVR Grantura

63C Vauxhall Victor Series II

63D Wolseley 15/60

INDEX

ABBREVIATIONS

bhp	brake horsepower
IFS	independent front suspension
OHC	overhead camshaft (engine)
OHV	overhead valves (engine)
PT	purchase tax
q.v.	*quod vide* (which see)

SUMMARY OF MAJOR BRITISH CAR MAKES
1955–59 (with dates of their existence)

AC	(from 1908)	MG	(from 1924)
Alvis	(1920–67)	Morgan	(from 1910)
Armstrong Siddeley	(1919–60)	Morris	(from 1913)
Aston Martin	(from 1922)		
Austin	(from 1906)	Riley	(1898–1969)
		Rolls-Royce	(from 1904)
Bentley	(from 1920)	Rover	(from 1904)
Bristol	(from 1947)		
		Singer	(1905–70)
Daimler	(from 1896)	Standard	(1903–63)
		Sunbeam	(from 1953)
Ford	(from 1911)		
		Triumph	(from 1923)
Hillman	(from 1907)		
Humber	(from 1898)	Vauxhall	(from 1903)
Jaguar	(from 1932)	Wolseley	(from 1911)
Lagonda	(1906–63)		

ACKNOWLEDGEMENTS

This book was compiled and written largely from historic source material in the library of the Olyslager Organisation, and in addition photographs were kindly provided or loaned by several manufacturers and organisations, notably:
AFN Ltd (Mr W. H. Aldington), Allard Owners Club Ltd (Mr David Kinsella), British Leyland UK Ltd, Chrysler UK Ltd, Ford Motor Company Ltd and Vauxhall Motors Ltd.